WHITE LUNG

KIMBERLY O'CONNOR

saturnalia | BOOKS

Distributed by Independent Publishers Group
Chicago

Saturnalia Books
105 Woodside Rd.
Ardmore, PA 19003
info@saturnaliabooks.com

ISBN: 978-1-947817-30-2 (print), 978-1-947817-31-9 (ebook)
Library of Congress Control Number: 2021938913

Cover art and book design by Robin Vuchnich

Distributed by:
Independent Publishing Group
814 N. Franklin St.
Chicago, IL 60610
800-888-4741

Acknowledgments

The poems below, some in different versions, were published in the following journals:

B O D Y: "Kali Kali Kali"

Cloudbank: "The History of My Silence (Late summer heat)"

Colorado Independent: "It's Okay" and "Untitled (By the end)"

Colorado Review: "The History of My Silence (begin anywhere)," The History of My Silence (white people sit in the front)," and "Thrush"

Harvard Review: "Letter to My Parents Explaining How I Became a City Person"

Passages North: "Clairvoyance"

Slice: "Early Pleistocene Horses"

storySouth: "My Grandmother Speaks"

Tar River Poetry: "Long Black Veil"

When a woman tells the truth she is creating the possibility for more truth around her.

—Adrienne Rich

Contents

WHITE LUNG

White Lung

It's some year:

1601, 1953, 2019,

2742. Plaster walls, pink roses. Laundry.

So much laundry. The cat hair

clings to it.

A red ant carries

its dead comrade over the wood chips.

Coughing.

The breath—

it cannot be caught.

The damp sheets move

in the breeze.

2019

INSERT torn out page

of a newspaper

smeared with toast butter smeared

with

sneeze drizzle

it says pulmonologist

Appalachia

it says coal dust it says radiologist

mountains mines

poverty

air arm/

chair

despair

it is scattered with crumbs

most of it is

illegible

1601

I'm drifting through roses.
I'm dying. I'm a witch
burning. Being burned.
INSERT flames.
I'm a bitch held down while
the men take their turns.
I'm a girl drifting
through clouds that feel
like roses. Flying.
INSERT rose petals.
Screaming.
I can't speak. I'm dying.
My body becomes
my daughter's body,
my granddaughters' bodies.
For centuries my cells
will play out their scheming
in the bodies of girls not
dreamed of yet, of girls
gathering roses
and coughing without knowing why.

1982

even as a little girl I feel how when

men enter the house they change

the house the women's softness shifts

it's not that we change

what we're doing cooking cleaning

laughing (the scent of bleach in scalding

water) it's that our attention doubles

itself so we can sense when the men

are going to speak & when

the men speak the air crackles

the women wait to hear it & then move about

fashioning the world as the men

have asked us to by speaking

2019

INSERT phone screen displaying

> *since 2016 3,000 cases of black lung*
> *radiologists may no longer diagnose*
> *pulmonologists that have worked for*
> *coal companies may or may not get*
> *their benefits cannot catch his breath*
> *cannot provide for his family*
> *cannot work cannot even walk*
> *in the garden without losing his breath*

1953

a woman is peeling an egg
it is a white woman it is me a white
egg with a perfect egg

heaviness a perfect symbol for
something first the violence of
cracking it one two three four

taps on the counter then her fingers
searching its surface for the fissure
that will release the largest

plate like a tiny continent so egg =
earth also egg = motherhood &
egg = breakfast when the egg is naked

she puts it on a white plate
she sprinkles it with white salt
she serves it to the white child

1984

The men are playful.
They will take me to the lake
if I asks them to but I can sense
(before I splash into the water
when they grab my body & toss it into the air)
the violence laying latent in their hands

1799

A girl is looking at a deer.
The deer is hanging upside down
from a rope tied to a branch.
The deer is bound just below
the back hooves. The front hooves
are loose in the breeze.
Blood from the deer's nose
pools below it in the dirt.
The girl's uncles & boy cousins
have shot this deer in the darkness
of early morning & brought it home
to hang here & bleed.

2018

INSERT a helium balloon

to symbolize the soul

to symbolize the shortage of helium

INSERT a manual describing the mining of helium

the manufacturing of helium

or otherwise explaining how helium is obtained

INSERT a bouquet of roses

she collects

the souls of her dead grandmothers around her body

like balloons like roses

she buys at grocery stores & displays in Mason jars

1989

The air is heavy with sports sadness. The father is watching the game; his team is losing. He is silent, staring at the television, but the hollers & cheers of the fans of the team her father hates fill their living room. She is sad for her father, who will return to work tomorrow wearing his team's colors.

1985

A cat will take the breath of a sleeping baby so the cat must sleep outside. When they move into a new house the cat comes in the backseat then it climbs onto the man's head while he is driving making the daughter shriek & the car swerve. Then the man stops the car & grabs the cat & slams its body into the trunk. She will not remember later exactly when they no longer had a cat.

2003

INSERT grease-stained
recipe card for her grandmother's
deer barbeque

except the grandmother

did not write things down

INSERT the grease stain

2019

It seems like a sin to write
about the self with all the suffering
outside the self but my self keeps

       persisting

THE HISTORY OF MY SILENCE

The History of My Silence

Denver, Colorado

Just when I relax into the illusion that I don't have to worry

                  (another white woman

wandering the aisles)

Rosemary bread

When I was young and miserable and pretty

                      (amusing myself with stray remembered lines)

                           Graying hair

          Dreamily

recalling my grandmother's diets:

                    the watermelon diet where all day you ate
              watermelon

                    the soup diet where all day you ate soup

(she'd still cook us whatever we asked for, French toast, gravy and biscuits, give
us a stick of butter to eat like a banana, a raw potato to gnaw, a cup half filled

with coffee, half with milk, all the sugar we wanted)

                              (Me and my skinny cousins with our pony-
             tails)

        Which is the kind of salmon you're supposed to buy?

In the mirrored back of the dairy case I see myself

                              fatter than

I used to be

             dirty flip-flops

                              *(She might have been pretty when she
             was younger*

is what I imagine people might be thinking)

(But no one is looking at me)

                wheat bread eggs yogurt

the kind of peanut butter that is not oily

organic   raspberries though it is not raspberry season

Or is it?

(People are being tortured at this very moment children are being beaten are dying in Children's Hospital what right do I have to be

gloomy
I am so fat with wealth)

I am nobody.

I smile at the clerk because I am supposed to smile.

I donate twenty-five cents from bringing my own bags to

something

I cross the parking lot at the crosswalk thinking two hundred dollars—what did I buy?

Organic peanut butter puffs, that's what

The kind of salmon you're supposed to buy

And a blue car runs the stop sign

The blue car does not see me, does not stop

And I have to decide whether to shout I am here

The History of My Silence

begin anywhere I am a little white girl in
a grocery store line my father eyes some Black
people and says low *boola boola* I know

this is wrong I keep quiet I don't know

why I laugh a little
he means to be funny I don't know yet
the word for hot feeling in my face is

shame I know it feels bad or I am

a little white girl in history a Klansman's
daughter dreaming of flames say the word
heritage I know I am

bad say the word plantation my family
owns slaves when I am bad
my father beats me say the word belt when the people he enslaves
disobey they are whipped by my father or
each other I learn to embroider I am good
at it

The History of My Silence

Hendersonville, North Carolina, 1961

white people sit in the front my great-grandmother
says my mother is angry
she wants to sit in the back

my mother is six years old
her first time on a bus
she wants to sit in the back

why? she stamps her foot

my great-grandmother does not answer the rest of the world
the boycotts the marches the fire
hoses let loose on children burning
crosses any of it does not
exist for them

they sit in the front like good white
women I think that

their silence their
compliance
has flowed into me
a river I have to swim
even as the water turns to flame

The History of My Silence

November 24, 2014

keep your eye on Ferguson
my mother texts the day
before my birthday I am
making breakfast

there could be unrest nationwide and I've heard
some Blacks are going to target any white they see

I eat my oatmeal
I type *I'm not worried about that* I erase it
I type *please don't text me this stuff*
erase it *I love you* I erase it

later when I call my mother I tell her we don't
need to be afraid

there is a pause she says *the first time I knew*
there was a such a thing as a Black person we were
in the car with Mama and she said shh here comes
 a n____ I was scared I didn't know what
that was I didn't know why
we had to be quiet

but she got quiet and watched
the Black man walk by and
in that second something
was passed down to her that would
later be passed down to me

My American Childhood in Reverse

My tiny revolution: at 30, I tell my parents they can't say *n____*
in front of my daughter. When they visit the city, they are afraid
of the subway, the crowds, the men soliciting change.
They try Thai food but tire of walking everywhere. One year,
I don't go home at all. When my parents call
to ask when I'm coming back for good, I am silent.

K, the only Black girl in our group, is silent
then cries when R chooses a song with the word *n____*
in it to be her "life theme song." I'm 21. Our college production is called
"As Soon as I Find My Voice." R is afraid
K won't like her anymore. K explains that for years
she's felt that word's sting. R changes

her song. Before I leave for college at 18, *you've changed*
my boyfriend tells me. I'm silent.
He's right: I do like using big words; for years,
I've looked forward to leaving. *That's n____*
music, mutters my father, whom my boyfriend fears,
the song blaring as he speeds away. When J calls

to ask me to the 9th grade dance, I don't call
back. Though he makes me laugh in math, I can't change
the rule that white girls date white boys. I'm 14 and afraid
I've hurt his feelings. From now on he's silent
in class. *This refrigerator looks like a n____'s*
my grandmother mutters as she cleans. The year

I turn 10, I get a Barbie Dream House. The year
I turn 8, I write in my diary *B didn't call.*
I get to take ballet. Yesterday, some n____
came to see Daddy's truck. The leaves are changing
colors. I like fall. On the school bus, I am silent
when C asks if she can touch my hair. I am afraid

of her. I want to ask to touch hers too but I'm afraid.
In the grocery checkout, 5 years old, I try to read headlines: *1983, Year*
of the—word I can't read—and fall silent
when my father casts his eyes to the side, calls
softly *boola, boola,* and grins at me. Searching for change,
my mother hisses *shh* and we go home.

Shame

All of the girls in my 5th grade class were invited to a birthday party for the other K__, the one who wasn't me. The other K__ was Black. The rest of the girls in our class were white. Our mothers didn't want to let us go, but because she couldn't stand the thought of anyone having no guests at her birthday party, my mother let me. One other white girl's mother let her go too. Our mothers, both of them, told us not to eat anything.

At the party, we were the only two guests from our class. Our mothers picked us up early. There must have been cake, balloons, presents, but I don't remember any of that. I think we decided it was okay to eat a few chips.

Something Worth Saying

Start with: I'm sorry.

I know what shame is.

A symbol: a woman biting an apple.

Another: a girl in a library.

A memory.

A girl diving into a lake.

In this dream she can breathe in water

and silence has no power.

She opens her mouth to speak.

*

She opens her mouth to speak

and silence has no power:

in this dream she can breathe in water.

A girl diving into a lake,

a memory,

another, a girl in a library.

A symbol: a woman biting an apple.

I know what shame is.

Start with: I'm sorry.

The History of My Silence
September–November 2008, Washington, DC

Late summer heat turns the city into dream space. When my mother says on the phone Obama's probably secretly Muslim, I can't quite hear her through the tunnel rush. She tells me a story from when I was a baby: alone in Huntsville, where my father had taken a job, she got lonely. She made a friend, a young Black woman in their building. They'd take me on long walks. One day a car slowed beside them, a face shadowed by cap rim, a voice: *I don't want to see y'all together no more.* The car sped up and disappeared.

"What did you do?"

"I stopped walking with her."

My grandparents called a certain kind of nut (a chestnut?) *n____toes,* and a certain part of Hendersonville *n____town.* Though it poisons its speaker and its receiver, *n____* is as common a word there as *winter* or *water.* In October, we give fifty dollars to boost the campaign's last-minute numbers. An Obama Biden sign arrives for our window. My eyes keep reading Osama Bin Laden. I avoid the newspaper. I try to write a letter to my mother: Why I'm Voting for Obama. Rational, fact-based, organized as a list.

We spend election night with my husband's co-workers. CNN beams the image of a slim reporter from Chicago into their New York studio "via holograph." We laugh, and dinner is catered, but my stomach hurts. I sit by myself on a straight-back chair. I'm lonely.

When Obama wins, it happens fast: though someone shouts he's won it all when he wins Ohio, I don't believe it until the words appear on the screen: *Barack Obama, 44ᵗʰ President.* They go directly, no commercial break, to McCain's concession. He silences some boos. I can't call my mother or my sister. People cry. It can't be real.

For the rest of November, on the Metro, I watch the trees burst like matches in slow motion and fade to rust. I watch workers put up and take down the fair beside the Hyattsville station, the one I like so much to see after evening classes, the children shrieking on the Ferris Wheel, colored lights streaking the sky. In the last three months, we could have started and lost a baby, or started one that lasted long enough to tell our families. If I had a baby, I could forbid certain things to be said in front of it. Whether or not anyone followed my wishes, my position on the matter would be clear.

Old Dominion

Remove arteries,
veins, and clotted blood
around heart

was the start of a recipe
for chicken pie in
a 1920's cookbook

I found and read in the house
of friends we were staying with
in Charlottesville. It was

an heirloom. Their whole house
was antique, old fashioned:
mason jars, strawberries

resting in colanders, milk
in a white porcelain pitcher.
Worn embroidered linen dishcloths.

She canned. He cut wood
for fires in winter but
this was summer. The air

almost tropical, unbreathable.
Azaleas. Wisteria. Roses.
When I breathed in, it hurt.

The house hurt me and
I didn't know why.
Everything was white.

Clotted blood around heart—
I wanted that cookbook.
I almost stole it. I was

a terrible houseguest. I wanted
to go home. I cried beside
the clawfoot bathtub

throughout the afternoon.
I wanted to go home and
I wanted to own that house.

The Gun in My Mother's Purse

When my mother was pregnant with me, two men tried to pull her from her car through the half-down window in a K-Mart parking lot. She got away. Her purse held a pistol my whole childhood. *Be careful with my purse* was one of her mantras. It had the bulk of an animal, came with her to recitals, teacher conferences, Chinese buffet lunches. It sat in the backseat under my sister's dangling feet.

Where was it I first learned that purse was slang for vagina? Chaucer? Middle school? A college friend whose mother hated the word? *Say pocketbook.*

BRIEF HISTORY OF WOMEN'S FREEDOM

Brief History of Women's Freedom

My grandmother didn't drive. She wouldn't learn. She had to be driven everywhere by my grandfather, her son, or one of her daughters. Her daughters tried to teach her. She was too scared to press the gas pedal. Imagine never going anywhere alone!

My mother left my father at least five times I can remember. We'd get in the truck with a few clothes thrown together and she'd speed away. Once we drove all night from the coast of North Carolina to the mountains. The lights on the dashboard were green and yellow. I slept with my head on my mother's lap.

Here in Colorado, when I back out our blue SUV from the garage, I am impressed with my ability to navigate tight spaces. But I won't drive in the mountains. The curves and big trucks terrify me. I feel no desire to go to the mountains alone.

Letter to My Parents Explaining How
I Became a City Person

1.
First, I lived in cities.

2.
Sitting beside the window this morning,
I hear the sound of soft rain, cars on the interstate,
birds in the bush next door, a train.

A helicopter now. My daughter's lingering
cough downstairs amid her toy computer songs
and a car swishing past on the wet street.

Sometimes Barky Joe, the name we've given
to the dog who barks and barks and barks
two doors down—and me the daughter

of you two, one of whom, according to
family mythology as well as my fuzzy memory,
punched a neighbor in the face because

her yappy dog kept you up
for most of your second pregnancy.
My sister was born in February.

The dog disappeared soon after.
I should be ashamed of myself,
listening for months—two years!—

to Barky Joe before someone *else* on our street
finally reports him and his owners shut him
behind a plywood gate they make for that purpose.

What I am trying to say is I like the noise.

3.
There is always somewhere to go.
Though I don't leave the house much
this summer, since I'm writing this
within blocks of three bookstores,
their brick walls lined with books
I haven't read yet, restaurants offering
basil fried rice, spicy tuna rolls,
gluten free pizza dough (though
I don't need it, we still eat wheat),
a store that sells dildos (though I've
never been inside). A Goodwill.
A fancy bowling alley. A fabric store.
Along the sidewalks, sometimes
homeless people, or crazy people,
or some combination of those
who require in passing a drawing up
of a certain kind of humanity:
generosity, at best, or at least
kindness in denial. Sometimes
drunk people, who sometimes talk or sing.

When you visited, this neighborhood
scared you. I don't like to be scared
either, so I like to live somewhere
a little bit scary. It's how I know I'll be okay.

4.
Does it make a difference that
we have a garden, albeit one scattered
in raised beds you're unsure of,

having gardened exclusively in rows?
Even if sometimes stray people
sidle by and take a few tomatoes,

once a whole pepper plant by the roots,
when I garden don't I hold
my grandmother's hands, your hands?

5.
When the trash truck comes
and my daughter dashes out the back door
to watch and I follow,

crossing my arms over my thin t-shirt,
the trash man does a kind of dance,
leaning in to take hold of the cans,

lifting them shoulder high,
flicking his wrist to turn them upside down.
They empty, and then he spins, almost

a twirl, to put each back in its place,
yells HEY and bangs the side of the truck,
runs like a deer to the next one.

It's beautiful and quick.
The alley smells like trash,
and I'm happy.

My Grandmother Speaks

I could eat them with a spoon the neighbor would say
every time he drove the tractor over and saw
the girls playing on the red dirt bank: they'd climb up
and up and slide down so fast they wore their palms
raw stopping. *Suppose there was a pageant among them,*
he said, *which one would win.* I snatched the corn

he'd brought to give and sent him on. That afternoon
I found two of them stripped to their panties, kneeling
over their toys, a naked Barbie on her back pressed
underneath a bear. *What are you doing,* I said, *keep
this door open.* My daughters' daughters. They blinked
and didn't say a word. Suppose there *was* a pageant—

dark-haired girls, all apple-cheeked, eyes green
as the lake. We put them in the fire truck
for the Apple Festival Parade: look at them wave
and toss down their candy. We should have found
a spoon while we could have done it. Now can't a single
one of them walk past a mirror without looking in it.

The History of My Silence
November 2016

The morning of the election I am combing lice from my daughter's hair, and we are watching a video of Hillary Clinton's last campaign ad set to Katy Perry's "Roar." I'm getting all teary saying to my daughter how nifty it'll be to have a woman president.

That afternoon we go to the park. Trump has leads in the early exit polls. No one is worried, but I am lonely. I text my mother and sister, *If Hillary wins will you at least be happy about the first woman president?* My sister does not answer. My mother says no.

We go home and order takeout. We turn on the TV. I do the lice combing. By the time I finish it's clear that we won't have a woman president. We keep watching in silence. Friends text and stop texting. We go to bed.

I used to bite my tongue and hold my breath are the first words of "Roar." It's a catchy song, one my daughter already knows from P.E. class. I take to listening to it in the car.

It's Okay

we judge each female body when we see it

(don't say you don't do it we all know

we all do it) here I am at a stoplight looking

at the woman walking her dog thinking

she's pretty she would be pretty if her belly

was a little firmer you can tell it's soft

by the way her t-shirt bulges like the way

my t-shirt bulges over the seatbelt

catching a glimpse of myself in the

window I am surprised I thought I was thinner

(this is a memory the ghost of me) and now

I notice two men are also watching

the woman she is pretending

it's not happening they are stopping

pointing calling they talk about

her body with each other

she keeps walking

it's hard to remember this used to happen to me

but I did walk down the hill

on Rosemary Street men's voices

saying *looking good sugar honey sweetie so*

sweet show us your stuff

I was thin terrified

the thing to do

was keep walking sometimes I'd smile a little

smile to show my tolerance

sometimes I kept my face so still

it looked like it wasn't happening sometimes they yelled

louder sometimes I walked a tiny bit faster not too fast

the thing was to pretend it wasn't happening

and it's okay now if the president says pussy

it's okay because boys will be boys girls will be

my daughter will grow up and walk on sidewalks

her body will be her shell her body will be her

downfall we will assign a number to it

her softness a space we will let

words bullet into *it's okay*

baby I'm just watching you walk by

Portrait of a Lady

her father an electrician her mother
a hairdresser (it's not that simple)
(you want her to be nice
and quiet) she's a girl reading
in her tiny bedroom in the trailer
she does not say a word

you don't want to read the word
*n*____ but there it is her mother
says it her father says it the trailer
echoes with its two-syllable
thud & poison you can read
(here) where she wrote it in her diary a nice

(straight white) girl straight hair straight A's nice
and quiet (like you want) says not a word
sits in the beauty shop reading
spinning a chair while her mother
cuts hair (she imagines she is special)
they drive the dirt road to the trailer

they move out of the trailer
build a house (big wood nice)
when her father wins a sweepstakes
they look at the letter repeating the words
over and over (it's true) her mother
gives her the letter to read

there it is in red
(one hundred thousand dollars) the trailer
becomes a memory her mother
moves the shop to the new nice
spare room the ladies get shampoo & styles words
hum white noise white ladies scissors

swish you can see it (it's simple)
a white girl grows up in the South its red
& pink mimosas dripping scent the words
they say there taking root trailing
tendrils in even nice
girls' minds (everyone says them even mothers)

Clairvoyance

My friend who is psychic says the soul's greatest hope is to enter a body. When a soul enters a body, it's thrilled. It's like the best thing that ever happened to a soul.

My other friend who is an accountant doubts this. She says it'd be better for a soul to be separate. Why would the soul want to deal with a body? A soul can't drink wine, I point out. We are at a wine bar. The soul can't run and jump, see colorful leaves—it's fall. She's not buying it. But I believe. My friend's friend who owns the wine bar brings us more wine, for free. *Pear*, she is saying, *honey*.

I tell the story of visiting my friend's clairvoyance class to our other friend. It's a real class, one I would like to join. They did a reading, not of my future, more like my present. My auras. Were they right? she asks. Well, they said I had a lavender rose, with one leaf. Leaves correspond to number of children so that's right.

They also said I had an outdated belief that women can't be powerful. Is that true? my other friend asks. It probably is. Around the same time I had a chance encounter with an Indian fortuneteller. Like from India? Yes. And she said in the fall I was going to get a new job, but I had to think big. Don't think about being in a fishbowl, the fortuneteller said, think about being in an ocean. That was before I visited the class. At the class they said I was swimming in scuba gear. And I was frustrated because I wasn't getting anywhere. Because what I couldn't see was that I was in a fishbowl. This is a good story, and true, but she looks skeptical.

I tell my other friend her hair is beautiful, and she gasps and covers her head with her hands. It's—she pauses—well, thank you, but we're going away next week, and after that there's my presentation, and I need to make an appointment. In the light of the wine bar, her hair looks like fire.

It's difficult, to love the body. It's difficult to live in the world. Already today I could tell you a hundred sad things. This year one of my students has a bruised face. I hope his soul is still happy to be with his body. I hope his life gets better so he can look back from the end and be happy. Like looking out the window of an airplane. The world growing smaller and bigger at the same time.

Long Black Veil

Ten years ago, on a cold dark night
Someone was killed, 'neath the town hall light
There were few at the scene, but they all agreed
That the slayer who ran, looked a lot like me

The judge said son, what is your alibi
If you were somewhere else, then you won't have to die
I spoke not a word, thou it meant my life
For I'd been in the arms of my best friend's wife

Oh, the scaffold is high and eternity's near
She stood in the crowd and shed not a tear
But late at night, when the north wind blows
In a long black veil, she cries ov'r my bones

She walks these hills in a long black veil
She visits my grave when the night winds wail
Nobody knows, nobody sees
Nobody knows but me

Handmade lace, dotted with pearls,
embroidered with vines and flowers,
maybe with fawns peeking
from a curtain of willows,
noses lifted, ears cocked.

Or something older,
passed down from a mother
or grandmother. Or something
cheaper—perhaps they were poor.
It doesn't matter—she found the veil,
and she made it black—

the girl from the song, I mean.
I always mix it up and think
it was her who *spoke not a word*,
but it was him. She just *stood
in the crowd and shed not a tear.*
Her silence was silent. Silenced.
She became a ghost. Ashes,
dry, breathable, firescraps pressing
the soft places below her kneecaps.
Ink from an inkwell,
ebony, consistency of milk or blood,
vinegar-scented. A bowl
of blackberries, holding them
one at a time between her thumb
and forefinger, pressing, juice
staining the veil, also her fingers,
her wrist: this is how
she turned the white veil black.

~

I imagine she lived in the woods,
the mountains. Although I want
the mountains, they're not mine.
I didn't grow up in them, just
under. My great-grandmother
tried to teach me to crochet, but
I wouldn't learn. She knew a storm
before its thunder by the way
leaves turned in the wind.
I remember that. Once I asked her
about my great-grandfather
who died before I was born.
Whatever she was doing, she stopped —
she was rarely still—*I didn't mean
to marry him*, she said. I laughed.
An accident, like missing
a step on the stairs. A bet
with her sister to see who could get a ring first.
Thinking she could break it later,
she accepted a proposal. But her beau arrived
in a borrowed car. She got in.
He didn't tell her
where they were going
till they got to the preacher's house.

~

I didn't wear a veil, having read
that the lifting of one by the groom
signified the bride as body
passing from father to husband.
For other brides, the veil is just
accessory, something pretty
to complement a ballerina skirt
and beaded bodice. Or the veil
is modesty, preserving the bride's
beauty for the groom alone. Norse brides
were kidnapped: a blanket thrown
over the head of a captured woman
secured and subdued her. Or veil as privacy.
A welcome place to watch.

~

Pearls, pearls,
in a haul
of three tons,
only three

or four pearls.
From the James
River, mussels?
Or the ocean,

oysters? Shapes:

round, button,
pear, circle,
drop;
          sizes:

opera,
princess,
collar,
choker,
rope.

                    ~

My mother's first marriage
was much like her grandmother's.
Seventeen, a high school senior,
her boyfriend dropped to one knee.
She laughed and said her father
wouldn't let her. For the honeymoon,
they drove to Disney World.
She called collect to tell her parents
they were safe, but her father
wouldn't accept the charges.
He didn't need to speak to her
to know that she was there.

~

And the woman from the song,
maybe she looked back
at her lover's body
hanging there, ripe peach
on a summer branch.

~

And after, did she live in the forest?
How then to keep the veil black?
Mud wouldn't be enough. The charcoal gills
of mushrooms, pulped roots of irises,
crushed hickory nut hulls.
Feathers the crows lost, tucked in
by their shafts to the lace.
Did she sleep on the ground?
Under elms? And once did
a shadowy moth land beside her
in the dusk? Its wings, if plucked
and smeared, a fine dark dust.

Bliss Body

My mother and aunts and my grandmother are washing the dishes,
the way they have washed the dishes after every meal, three times
a day seven days a week every week of all the years they are
alive to wash the dishes while the men sit outside and smoke,
and when I am old enough to help rinse the dishes under
the scalding water my grandmother insists that we use,
what I remember about washing the dishes is the way
despite everything, they always start laughing, they get tickled,
as my grandmother says, one of them says something funny
and the laughter catches on, one by one they start laughing,
each aunt in turn, my mother, my grandmother, the laughter
spreads like fire and the rest of us, the girls cousins helping
wash the dishes, we start laughing too, even when we don't know
what's so funny, all of us laughing, washing the dishes laughing
till we can't stand, laughing till we cry, till we we're gasping for breath

Roe v. Wade

The facts of anything

are tangled and particular.

Who *was* Roe? Wade?

Realizing I didn't know

what I was so upset about

when I got upset about Roe v. Wade,

I turned to books.

Not true.

I googled it.

*

The facts of anything

unravel at your touch.

The facts unspool and unspool.

*

It turns out Roe was Jane Roe, a fake name for Norma McCorvey. Norma
McCorvey worked selling tickets at a traveling show. Norma McCorvey was
raped after the show one night. The facts unspool: youth, abuse, poverty, despair.
Abortions were illegal in Texas. She could have gotten an illegal abortion, but
she had no money, and she was afraid.

*

In one book about Norma,
she was raped; in another
which happens to be
her memoir, she lies
and *says* she was raped
thinking that if
she was raped, she'll
find someone to do
the abortion. In this version,
after having two children,
she has just found out
what abortion is,
that it even exists.

*

The American Medical Association wrote that a woman who wanted an abortion was

unmindful of the course turned out for her by Providence.

*

At the Supreme Court during the arguments for Roe v. Wade there were

no ladies bathrooms in the lawyers' lounge.

*

I am afraid and very selfish
of this story: a new
mother, who is me,
who feels nothing like
the me I used to be,
decides to take the baby
(for months she is only
the baby, nameless; though
we did name her, she is
a sea creature, expression-
less, helpless, a vortex)
to a coffee shop across
Capitol Hill in D.C.,

(where we lived then) so
I have to push the stroller
past the Supreme Court
and through the haze
of exhaustion I the new mother
now live in I realize that
everyone is smiling at me
and then that they are all
holding signs and then
that there are hundreds of them
smiling at me and holding signs
and then I begin to read what
the signs say: *One Life*
Taken, Many Hearts Broken;
Abortion Stops a Beating
Heart; I am a Pro-Life
Feminist; I Regret My Abortion
and as I read the signs
a rage that is like
a match being struck ignites
deep in the fog of me:
they are smiling at me
because of the baby.

*

Sherri Finkbine

      read the newspaper
      loved children
      starred in a children's show called Romper Room
      had four children of her own

read in the newspaper

      babies had been born
      babies had been born in Europe
      babies had been born in Europe with just

heads and torsos

Their mothers had taken sleeping pills called thalidomide. Two facts were true:

1. Sherri Finkbine was pregnant.

2. Sherri Finkbine had taken thalidomide.

Sheri Finkbine

      called her doctor

Her doctor

recommended abortion

Sherri Finkbine wrote

to a hospital panel

who approved the abortion

and here the facts

unspool and unspool: hoping to save other women, Sherri calls a newspaper. The press scares the hospital. The hospital revokes their approval for the abortion. The Finkbines sue the hospital. The pregnancy progresses. The babies being born with hands and feet attached to their torsos are named "thalidomide babies." The Finkbines go to Sweden. After several days of examinations and the review of a medical board, Sherri gets an abortion. The fetus is deformed. The Finkbines go home where they receive multiple death threats. The television network replaces Sherri as their Romper Room host

due to publicity over the ordeal.

*

The question is whether

a woman has the right

to decide whether or not

to carry a pregnancy to term.

Whether a woman

has the right

to kill her baby is

another way to say it.

When my baby was a baby, I'd say to anyone who listened

if I got pregnant again right now I'd have an abortion.

                *

A Joke

Does giving birth hurt?

Yes, and then your life is ruined.

*

Things that have happened to abortion providers:

> stalking
> home picketing
> business loss
> death threats
> community protests
> racial attacks
> religious attacks
> hate mail
> targeted Internet postings
> arson
> assault
> murder

*

The facts of anything

are tangled and particular.
When someone first told her
she could get an abortion, Norma McCorvey
didn't know what abortion was.

*

The first abortion doctors
were medicine women
or witches later burned at the stake.

Hot Mamas

Cheerleading tryout flashbacks & the mirror

tells me I'm not going to make it.

All the women here are white

& wearing black stretch pants.

INSERT photo that appears when Hot Mama's

app is opened: white lady's torso shaped

like an hourglass, belly's curve concave,

hipbones jut. No face. The teacher says

get a strap, block, mat, three-pound

weights. INSERT photo of four

white women at a ballet barre.

The music calls us bitches.

Says bend over. Says shut up.

Says keep going. Without

the music we could not keep going.

INSERT song lyrics: *Mask on. Fuck it,*

mask off. I have a crush on the teacher.

INSERT photo of the teacher: blonde, 5'2",

XS, skull tattoo on her defined bicep.

I like to think the teacher is watching me.

Of course the teacher is watching me:

it's her job to watch. We all like to think

someone is watching us. Someone is

always watching us. INSERT list

of Hot Mama's class offerings:

Sexy Sweat, Meet Me at the Barre,

Kick Your Asana, Skinny Jeans,

Sweatin' Like a Mutha. Every wall here

is a mirror. I am pretty sure the teacher

does not like me. I am pretty sure

I am pretty enough. *I am pretty*

is something we are all trying to think

& think that others are thinking when

they see us. That we are all white

means something we don't have to

think about too much. We will all go home

and complain about having to make dinner.

Dinner will make us fat. Dinner's relentlessness

will make us forget our incredible luck.

I drive to Whole Foods to get

something to make for dinner.

Mirrors line the Whole Foods' dairy case.

INSERT Whole Foods receipt. Photo of

a half-gallon of organic milk.

Gentrifier

Your mind wants to submit evidence against the fact of it:

the trailer you grew up in, the outhouse your mother
shat in as a child,

that one-room shack that stands in for the poverty

your grandparents endured.

The winter wind wailing through thin, split walls. The table bare. Maybe a bean or two.

Yet when you sell your house for a hearty profit
to the white couple whose parents are helping them buy it

you know

that whatever reasons you had for coming here or leaving here
the case was settled before your birth.

The call west was a call to colonize.

That despite the blood of the enslaved that must be in your veins, in this particular body
the slave-owner's blood there prevailed

to create a body (dotted with brown though it may be)

("freckles")

more white than anything else.

Created a white body.

The white body watched the neighbors disappear.
The white body dreamed distantly of desert massacres.
The white body devoted its career to—

trying to do something

        "good"—

as though that could be an —

amendment. Could be proof of a good heart.

As though history could be amended.

The sin is the skin color, the heritage, your albatross.

It can't be put down.

KALI KALI KALI

Kali Kali Kali

for Clayton Lockett, died April 29, 2014
for J.V. Brown, died March 7, 2014
for Iris, who was never born

Kali descended and asked me
to describe her in three words.
I said goddess of destruction.

She said goddess of time and
change. I said that's five words.
She said I can't be contained.

In a circle, there is no end and
no beginning. If we assume now
we are in a circle, there is nowhere

to begin. Let's begin with it is morning
and I am standing on the sidewalk
at the center of a thousand colors,

a thousand textures: silk and brittle,
petal and spike, wrapping paper,
burst balloons blown over from a party

the wind ended, the tree's shed leaves,
dog shit, flowers, a spectrum
of greens. Or, three things happened:

My grandfather died. My best friend
had an abortion. The state of Oklahoma
executed Clayton Lockett.

Or, at the coffee shop the silverware
clatters to the floor, and the toddler
who has climbed back into

the chair she just fell out of
falls out again. Or rather, the chair
topples over, not once but twice,

then a third time, and the girl cries
all three times, and her nanny puts her
in her stroller and they leave.

The manager asks me if I saw
what happened. That chair is slippery,
I say, or maybe it's the floor.

Some things seem bound to
keep happening over and over
as the rest of us watch, astonished.

Or we can begin with before
the abortion, when the government made my friend
google *seven weeks pregnant*

and look at the photos,
the hands and feet paddles,
the heart a center darkness.

~

Or, let's make a list. Wars, of course.
Count the wars: one, two, three,
four. And disease: Ebola. Enterovirus D68.
Whooping cough. What else. Airstrikes,
or not. Peace protests, or not. Coal ash.
Radiation in the drinking water. The woman
in Liberia whose whole family died,
and now her village shuns her because—
but I already said Ebola. The woman
who was held hostage for 11 years,
kept in a cage, who bore and cradled
the child of her captor. The woman
who, the woman who. Wars. The daughter
of the woman whose boyfriend beat her
to death signs up for a writing class
about grief. My daughter gets a cough
and a bee sting. I call the 24-hour Walgreen's.
The wars are far away. The man with the sign
that says *Vietnam Vet, Anything Helps*
is always on the corner of our block.
I turn down the music when I pass

and hand him packs of trail mix, or
I'm out of trail mix so I wave and don't turn down
the music, or I don't wave and try not to look.
I have said all this before. The pharmacist
says five-year-olds can take Benadryl.
What a miracle the 24-hour Walgreens is.
I would lie down on the floor
in thanks but I have to make breakfast.

~

Or we can begin in a dream in which
I am explaining to an audience
the concept of the karmic circle:

my actions affect your actions. It's a snake
swallowing its tail. It's a ring of flame,
that old symbol. Or I am saying

in a voicemail to my friend the way
the sun is filling the trees this morning
is a trick. We have to steel ourselves

against it. Dead bee in a zinnia,
the zinnia browning but still pink,
the bee a frozen model of itself.

~

But I am not talking about
any of that. I am talking about
myself and my own little griefs.
I am talking about griefs
I witnessed or witnessed someone
else witness. I am not talking
about innocence. I am talking about
the moment my friend swallowed
the pill against the sound of
her own voice saying no.
I am talking about the times
I saw her name on my phone's
screen and didn't pick up because
I couldn't take any more pain.
I am talking about the death
of my grandfather which was
the death of a family. I am not
talking about that at all.
I am talking about a specific
murder that happened years ago
and the final, violent closing
of that circle. I am talking about
a handmade noose of sheets.
No, I am talking about my own
death and my dread of it. No,
I am talking about standing
at the abyss of it, witnessing.

~

The prisoner led from
his cell to his death
in the name of all of us.

After the execution,
I stopped listening to
the news. It was a great excuse

since I don't like the news.
The audience is raising its
collective hand and saying *but*:

he was a murderer. But I'm
not talking about innocence.
There are a thousand ways

to talk about what happened.
Let's talk about rattling
the bars. When an inmate is led

from the cell block to the execution chamber,
the other inmates rattle the bars.
Rattle the bars with what?

I don't know.
Hardback books? Spoons?
Their bare hands?

Whatever will make noise.

~

On the sidewalk I talk
to Kali: Kali when she
swallowed the pill that
would end the baby's life
Kali when he steeled
his face against death
Kali when I bought
the flight to the funeral
Kali when they pulled
the curtains closed
Kali when she couldn't
bury the body Kali when
we stood at the grave
and couldn't cry: really?
All this will happen again?

~

After my grandfather died his mouth
hung open as if he was astonished
at his own absence. After the execution,

I stopped listening to the news.
Instead now, in the mornings, I walk
around the block and talk to Kali:

Kali because of you
the sidewalk is scattered
with ribbon and petals and glass.

Untitled (By the end)

By the end, we won't remember what
happened when. We'll remember hardly
any of it. The only thing that makes it

bearable is all the blossoming. The trees
turn white, then green. What unfolds
for me unfolds secondhandedly.

While they're injecting the midazolam,
I am watching little white girls in black
leotards play tag. Or it takes longer

than I think and we are already driving
home for dinner. But let's go back
to before that. There was a murder.

It was violent. It was not an accident.
A young white woman died and a young Black man
went to prison. Elsewhere, unrelated,

I want to be a poet. I fall in love with
someone. He becomes a lawyer.
We become a mother and a father.

We move to Denver. My husband meets
the young man in prison. He's no longer
young. He becomes a kind of friend.

Of course this takes years. I learn
things like in supermax, the inmates
are required by law to have access

to one hour of sunlight per day.
The light through a skylight counts.
The men can't touch their families

or each other. The day before their
executions, their mothers cannot hug
their sons good-bye. No one cares about this.

Why should they? Their victims' parents
didn't get to hug their children before—
yes. That is correct. So what's wrong

with me? My husband sends his client books.
Should I say his name? He likes
vampire books. Mysteries. Thrillers.

When my husband calls him with the news
that the last appeal has been denied,
Clayton says *Have a good weekend*

when they hang up. My husband
flies to Oklahoma City. I wait.
My daughter's dance class is in a church.

I sit in the sanctuary and imagine
I am holding Clayton's hand.
I am ridiculous. But my hand feels

warm for a minute. My husband calls
and he is weeping. Or he is furious.
He's not dead yet, he says.

*They kicked us out. They closed
the curtain and they made us leave.*
It's the end of April, everything's in bloom.

It snows, then the sun comes back.
By summer, we should feel better.
By autumn, we might forget.

Our garden grows. We harvest. I walk
through the alley carrying vegetables.
When I get home and dump out the cucumbers,

I'm filled suddenly with joy. I pirouette
around the kitchen and imagine Clayton
is dancing with me, his spirit, anyway.

I think he is. I wish for it. I imagine
his victim's mother wishing deeply
for my death, and I don't blame her for it.

If When

if when I read the news that a person whose name I did not know
whose name will now be famous
will be forever spoken with fathomless grief
I am wearing a black dress

if when I say person I mean Black man
if when you read person you think or don't think
Black man

if when I keep reading I can't stop crying
or can't cry or am unable to keep working
or keep working if I am paralyzed

if I keep working when I see the video
if I watch it or don't watch it if when
I read the words I am right here with you mommy
I want to vomit

if I am wearing a black dress if
I am a white woman if I have forgotten
the names if you remember the names

if I list words from the news stories police
Minneapolis federal inquiry multiple gunshot
wounds cafeteria supervisor protestors weeping

if you throw rocks riot control snipers
multiple gunshots protestors video sir Dallas
Baton Rouge nephew brother son mother child

if the police stop you comply say sir

if the police say sir weeping

if I list the names or don't list the names

if the list of names is too long to list

if the list could fill a thousand pages longer

if when this happens I write this will I have done anything

worth doing will I do anything

If I Am Killed in a Mass Shooting

I could have been anywhere
I was there I am a daughter of
this country I hot rolled my hair

my high school history teacher
was a football coach we never got past
the Civil War the boys had gun racks

in their trucks the deer they hunted hung upside down
dripped blood that formed a pool we shredded their
flesh it made good barbeque

there is a feeling you are being watched
you glance over your shoulder
you light a candle in a vigil

I am a ghost
we are ghosts glancing backwards looking for
men with guns

know that I wrote this not to call it in but as
a way to ward it off
a lucky charm

people cry people cover people with blankets
flowers cover the sidewalks like
blankets the flowers fade to dust

do with me whatever you want
America I am yours

A: Light

Me (standing naked after a shower): What difference does it make, one person's story?

White lady yoga teacher, paraphrasing ancient yogis: Dark mind, ensnared in its own ugliness

Song playing in grocery store: Well I met you at the blood bank/we were looking at the bags

Red candle shaped like a lotus: [double flickers in the mirror]

Child's eyes (brown, green, blue): [opening before dawn]

White lady yoga teacher, paraphrasing ancient yogis: Busy mind makes heartbeat too fast

Sun on snow: [blinds drivers as the highway curves east toward the airport]

Desert shadows: [lengthen, shorten, disappear, lengthen, shorten, disappear]

Child's notebook: I forgot to tell you I am the hero

White lady yoga teacher, paraphrasing ancient yogis: full moon mind over still lake

Bathroom skylight (dotted with dead bugs): [illuminates the roiling steam]

The History of My Silence

The coal miner dreams about the boulder that crushed him

My insistence on walking around the block each morning

The yellow leaves all mixed up in the snow

The cat kills a mouse, then curls on the heat vent

He wakes up struggling to breathe

Is an insistence of the beauty of each day despite

The mouse is the size of my thumb and looks soft

He spends days in his armchair counting down

My daughter cries when I scoop it with a dustpan and walk outside

The three-degree weather and the death of everything

He says he will take it day by day till his kids graduate high school

Then

The truth is I am the big disaster

The tiny whiskers quiver in the cold

Early Pleistocene Horses

So long ago it can't be properly spoken of,
I was there and a human in it, a woman.
Ice stretched so far and wide the horses
had hardly any room to run. The horses ran
on ice. I rode them nightly in the ice air
though my father told me not to. My hair,
of course, streamed behind me like
the horses' tails. We were cold all the time.
I was the great-great-grandmother of Eve.
Even older than that. The horses were wild.
I did what I wanted and died very young
like everyone did. The sunrise was cold
as the sunset and noon was no warmer.
There were no words, though, for these:
noon, sunshine, wild horses. There was
only my breath visible in the wind
all the time, the live thing underneath me,
holding me up, the live thing beating in my body,
in time, these things happening in time,
for the short bright time they lasted.

Thrush

From the French, *fourchette,* the frog
of a horse's foot. Songbird, a robin
or blue one, brown-backed with
breast spots. Or a kind of whitish rash.

The frog of a horse's foot—hooves
in the west pasture, hoarse chorus
surging from the marshes. Or bird,
a thrash in the shadow of brambles

edging the threshed field; a blue one,
or the robin, brown-backed, bright breast,
calls from the willow branches. Wind
wet in the shallow grasses, hoarse

chorus surging from the marshes, thrash
in a tangle of brambles, spring shower
splashing down. Rising creek rushing.
Over the creekbed, passing shadow,

cabin window. Spring downpour, then
the drowning. Then the drying, thrush
in the mouth or the branches. And flash of
the spade, silver, thrust in the damp pasture.

Notes

This book's epigraph is from Adrienne Rich's *On Secrets, Lies, and Silence: Selected Prose.*

The fifth line of "The History of My Silence (Denver, Colorado)" is from Randall Jarrell's "Next Day."

"Long Black Veil" is the title of a song written by Danny Dill and Marijohn Wilkin in 1959 and performed by Johnny Cash and many other musicians since. The books *Wedding Dress Across Cultures; The Veil: Women Writers on Its History, Lore, and Politics; Jewels and the Woman;* and *The Frank C. Brown Collection of North Carolina Folklore* informed the poem.

Clayton Lockett, to whom "Kali Kali Kali" is partially dedicated, was my husband's legal client.

The third line of "A: Light" quotes Bon Iver's song "Blood Bank."

Acknowledgements

Thanking each person who helped a book 11 years in the making is impossible. This list could be a thousand pages long. But I will try.

So first, thank you to all my teachers, both formal and informal, including Chuck Sullivan, my very first poetry teacher at North Carolina Governor's School in 1996; Alan Shapiro, Michael McFee, and Jim Seay, who encouraged me as an undergrad at UNC; Stan Plumly, Liz Arnold, Josh Weiner, Michael Collier, Martha Nell Smith, and Maud Casey at UMD, where I spent three glorious years as an MFA student; and to all the instructors I've worked with at Lighthouse Writers Workshop, including Chris Ransick, Elizabeth Robinson, Jen Denrow, and Jenny Wortman, for keeping my spirits up during the years I rewrote and revised this manuscript.

Thank you to John Brehm for treating me as a colleague when I wondered if I was a poet at all; to Major Jackson for giving me the courage to write about race; and to Jovan Mays for reading and workshopping some of those early poems with love and generosity.

To Ali Sweeney and Andrea Bobotis, thank you for unending support and cheerleading. Without you, I would have quit writing years ago. Thanks too to my teachers and peers at Karma Yoga Studio in Denver for love and light as I worked to publish this book, and to Judi Terrill, a healer who continues to help me find the courage to speak.

Deep gratitude to my colleagues at Lighthouse Writers Workshop, both present and past, especially to Mike Henry and Andrea Dupree for creating a family-friendly workplace that nurtures thousands of writers, including myself; Laurie Wagner for years of honesty and encouragement; and Roxanne Banks Malia, my work wife and a true soul mate. And thank you, truly, to the hundreds of other writers I've had the pleasure of knowing at Lighthouse through workshops, events, and readings, for sharing your own stories and listening to mine.

To Saturnalia Books and all the people behind the press: thank you, thank you, thank you for giving this book a home and bringing it into the world.

To Dean, my husband and best friend, I can't offer enough thanks for more than 20 years of unwavering support—and for telling me not to worry about contest submission fees.

Thank you to my daughter, Amelia, whose free and generous spirit is a daily inspiration.

And last, thank you to my family, especially my mother, who told me I could write whatever I want.

KIMBERLY O'CONNOR is a North Carolina native who lives in Golden, Colorado. Kim is the Young Writers Program Co-Director for Lighthouse Writers Workshop. She received an MFA from the University of Maryland. She has taught creative writing and literature in middle school, high school, and college classrooms in Colorado, Maryland, West Virginia, and North Carolina. Her poetry has been published in *B O D Y, Copper Nickel, Colorado Review, Harvard Review, Mid-American Review, Slice, storySouth, THRUSH,* and elsewhere.

White Lung is printed in Adobe Caslon Pro.
www.saturnaliabooks.org